WORLD RELIGIONS

WORLD RELIGIONS

By F. G. Herod

ARGUS COMMUNICATIONS   Niles, Illinois

PHOTO CREDITS

Warren Garst/TOM STACK & ASSOCIATES   72 top
Hersch Green/TOM STACK & ASSOCIATES   48
Jean-Claude LeJuene   9,17,25,32
Sue Moser   52,57
T.L. Ramaswamy/TOM STACK & ASSOCIATES   72 bottom
Lu Ming Sheng/TOM STACK & ASSOCIATES   64
Regina Simon/TOM STACK & ASSOCIATES   13
Tom Stack/TOM STACK & ASSOCIATES   44
TOM STACK & ASSOCIATES   68
Eric L. Wheater/TOM STACK & ASSOCIATES   4,29
Robert Wick/TOM STACK & ASSOCIATES   40

Printed in the United States of America
International Standard Book Number 0-913592-28-5
Library of Congress Number 75-18971

   2   3   4   5   6   7   8   9   0

CONTENTS

INTRODUCTION

This book is about the major religions of the world and what they have in common. It is written because of the widespread belief that, though we may belong to one particular faith, our knowledge of it is enriched by some knowledge of other religions; we ought to know what they too have to say about the great problems of human conduct and existence. Why are we here? To what end are we going? What kind of living is most worthwhile? What is the nature of that being whom people call God, or Yahweh, or Allah, or Brahman, or the Tao, and how should we worship Him or It.

"In my father's house there are many mansions." If we apply this saying to the religions of the world, we see that some are large and some are small. Some are small in the sense that they have not grown very much; and this book does not describe primitive religions devoted to the warding off of evil spirits and the pleasing of minor gods. For these make no attempt to answer those larger problems. There are other religions that may be profound but that are small in the sense they are not widespread, such as Jainism in India which has only two million followers, or Zoroastrianism in both Iran and India, which has fewer. For reasons of space only, such minority religions have not been included here.

There is also Communism, which, whatever one thinks of it, has many of the characteristics of a religion. It has its holy books, its prophets and fanatics, its dogmas and heresies, its prospects of paradise and its millions of believers. But its dogmas are about the means of life, not the end; and its paradise, if it ever comes, is strictly confined to the world around us. In that sense it too is small, and so is not discussed here.

There are many people who find themselves unable to accept any religion at all. If they believe definitely that there is no God, they are called *atheists*. If they feel that we simply cannot know anything for sure, they are best described as *agnostics*, which means *not knowing*. Or they may prefer to be called *humanists*, which means that the only values we can rightly have are those to do with human life and the best way of improving it. Such people have often thought very deeply about religion, and have religious feelings, but not the actual beliefs that enable them to practice it. This book will be of as much interest to such sincere people as to those who already belong to a faith but wish to view it in the larger perspective offered here.

The major world religions can be divided into three groups, all of which had their beginnings in the East. One group comes from the *Near East* and can be called Semitic. These religions in historical order are: Judaism, Christianity, and Islam. Judaism, by far the oldest, formed the basis for the other two religions. "I have come," said Jesus Christ," "to fulfill the Law, not to destroy it." And Muhammad, the founder of Isalm, accepted the Bible as an earlier revelation of Allah and looked on his religion as a fulfillment of the earlier two.

These three religions, therefore, share similar ideas and ways of looking at things: they are all *monotheistic*, that is they believe in only *one* God. They think of Him in personal terms as a fatherly being who created the world as something quite separate from Himself. God made man in His own image, gave him commandments to observe and told him to live in brotherly love with his fellowmen. The world He created is a good one, and man may have fallen from grace but can achieve salvation in spite of his fall. With this and much else in common, it is tragic that Jews, Christians, and Moslems should persecute and fight one another as they have so often done throughout the ages.

The second group of religions came originally from India. These are, in historical order, Hinduism, Buddhism and Jainism,

6

and much later the religion of the Sikhs. Hinduism, like Judaism, was not founded by a single person but developed gradually over many hundreds of years. Similarly, the religions which derived from it *were* founded by single people who did not attempt to convert others to their beliefs. The *derivative* religions on the other hand did seek to expand and to make converts. Christianity, Islam, and Buddhism became missionary religions which spread to far parts of the world, and in the case of Christianity and Buddhism almost died out in the actual lands of their birth.

But there the resemblance between Hinduism and Judaism ends. The Hindu way of looking at things is quite different. God is not thought of as a personal being who created a world separate from Himself. *Brahman* is thought of as something of which the whole universe is an expression. He is not a distinct God with a single face, but a being with infinite aspects. He can be worshiped in the form of many different gods and godlings, some good and some bad, some noble and some destructive. Life as such is not in itself good, and the final aim of a holy man is so to free himself of all earthly desires as to be able to return to that universal spirit from which he came in the first place.

However, we do not have only one life on earth in which to achieve this. The Hindus believe in *reincarnation*. They believe that the soul returns again and again to live in a different body, sometimes in a higher and sometimes lower form. So if at first a person worships stone idols daubed in paint then this must be allowed, for in his next reincarnation he may understand the Truth at a higher level. At last, after many lives, through self-discipline and spiritual contemplation, a soul may achieve release from the earthly cycle of desire and the suffering which goes with it. Then he can achieve unity with Brahman.

Buddhism branched away from Hinduism, and Jainism is an attempt to combine both. There are many differences between these three Indian religions, but they share to a large extent the same beliefs and attitudes towards life. The religion of the Sikhs is a result of the contact between Hinduism and Islam—which came to India from the West a thousand years after Christ and had great influence there.

The third group of major world religions is of the *Far East:* China and Japan. Buddhism started in India, as we have seen, but today there are only three million Buddhists still left there. Buddhism expanded outwards and became one of the major religions of the Far East instead. Those religions which actually began in China itself are Confucianism and Taoism.

Confucianism, which dates from the sixth century B.C. concerns itself less with the worship of God or the nature of the Ultimate Reality than with the conduct of people towards one another—towards parents, teachers, ancestors, and the authorities. It tolerated and improved the existing ceremonies of the people, but it was far more interested in the means of obtaining social harmony. This is because, at the actual time Confucius was teaching, China was going through a period of great civil unrest. The result was that he laid great stress on education, obedience, and self-effacement, and little on man's spiritual needs.

As if to compensate for this, there also developed in China the religion of Taoism, founded by a legendary old man called Lao-tzu. He did not imagine a God in the Judaic sense, but as a universal life force called the Tao. The Tao also means "The Way." Like all the great religions, but with more emphasis, Taoism teaches a humble and peaceful way of life that avoids ambition, greed, hurry, or discord. A man should respect life, human or animal. He should interfere with others as little as he should be interfered with. He should seek for harmony with the natural forces around him. Like water, he should try and find his own level, and achieve gentle contentment in his own life.

In China, Confucianism, Buddhism, and Taoism have existed together peacefully for centuries, molding in different ways the Chinese character. Further west, a person tends to think of himself as either Christian, Jewish, or Moslem, but in the Far East there is no feeling that a single faith provides the only means of salvation. Until recently in China, a man had three different religious traditions to choose and profit from.

Similarly, in Japan there are both Buddhism and Shinto. (There is also the Zen sect of Buddhism which has elements of Taoism in the same way the religion of the Sikhs combines Hinduism and Islam.) Shinto, like Confucianism, does not really attempt to probe the great problems of human existence or provide large answers. It developed in some isolation and has never spread outside of Japan. It is *animistic,* that is it invests natural things like trees and water with spirits which are both feared and loved. Because of this it has given rise to the unusual reverence the Japanese have for nature, and also to many beautiful ceremonies.

Shinto during the first half of this century was turned into a state religion devoted to the worship of the emperor; it was designed to support the authority of the very nationalistic government then in power. The attitudes it helped arouse led to the cruelties and disaster of the Second World War in the Far East, and Shinto fell into some disrepute as a result. However, it must be remembered that all the great religions have gone through their bad periods; their followers have often failed utterly to live up to the ideals behind them and the basic teachings of their founders. The moral teachings of all developed religions have been directed towards humility, sincerity, pacifism, and the love of one's brother, whatever the differences of emphasis and the different ideas of the nature of God or the meaning of life. That these ideals have been so constantly ignored is often used as an argument against religions in general. On the contrary it forms the best arguments for studying them in more detail—in all their richness and variety this book describes.

Jeremy Trafford

HINDUISM 1

Verily, the whole world is BRAHMAN. This soul of mine within the heart is smaller than a grain of rice or a barley corn or a mustard seed; this soul of mine within the heart is greater than the earth, the atmosphere, the sky, greater than these worlds.

Containing all works, all desires, all odors, containing all tastes, encompassing this whole world—this is the soul of mine within the heart, this is BRAHMAN. Into him shall I enter on departing hence.

Hindu Scriptures

Just within the jungle, sheltered from the burning heat of the sun, sits a young man, still and silent. His legs are crossed beneath him, his hands upon his knees and his head erect. So light is his breathing that you could hardly believe him to be alive. His eyes, apparently closed, are in fact concentrated on the tip of his nose. He is one of the holy men of India, and in this way he meditates for many hours each day.

Holy men are a common sight among the 430 million Hindus in India. Some remain all their lifetime in the jungle, others wander about the country, while others are to be found in the great temples. A genuine holy man is regarded with reverence, and many Hindus would feel honored to provide him with food or even pay his fare when he makes a journey by train.

The young man we have described is a *Yogi*, that is, he practices *Yoga*, a very severe form of self-discipline. The Hindu scriptures give a Yogi these directions:

The Yogi planteth his own seat firmly upon a spot that is undefiled, neither too high nor too low, and sitteth upon the sacred grass which is called Kusha, covered with a skin and a cloth. There he, whose business is the restraining of his passions, should sit with his mind fixed on one object alone, keeping his head, his neck and body steady without motion, his eyes fixed on the point of his nose, looking at no other place around.

Following these directions, Yogis gain remarkable control over their bodies, sometimes remaining in one position for days on end. They can hold their breath for long periods of time and are said to be able to control all the organs of their bodies, even the beating of their hearts.

They perform these strange exercises in order to disappear forever from the world. At the heart of Hinduism there is the belief that the physical world is an illusion: one day we may wake up to discover that it has all been a bad dream. There is no reason or purpose in what goes on around us. Day and night, summer and winter, birth and death roll on from one millennium to another with meaningless monotony.

Only one thing is real and unchanging—*Brahman*, the universal spirit, of which the soul of every living creature is a part. *"This soul of mine is greater than the earth, the atmosphere, the sky, greater than these worlds. . . .This is Brahman. Into him shall I enter on departing hence."*

A few years ago an American psychiatrist, Morey Bernstein, wrote a book entitled *The Search for Bridey Murphy*. In it he describes how a young American woman under hypnosis revealed that, before her present life, she had, in fact, lived another one. She gives a detailed account of it from her childhood in Cork in Southern Ireland to her death in Belfast. On investigation, some of the facts she gives have been verified, and if what she says is true it provides evidence that a human being can live more than one life on earth.

This, in fact, is what all Hindus believe. We live countless lives on earth. Our bodies are like suits of clothes. When one is worn out we discard it and take another. This process is called reincarnation. The Hindu Yogi believes that these endless births

and deaths are useless and full of suffering. He must break the cycle of reincarnation and return to Brahman forever. A life devoted to Yoga, he believes, will do this.

Only a few people in India can give their lives to Yoga, so they must be content with the next best thing: That when they return to this world again they will be better off. But to be better off, for a Hindu, is not to have more money but to be born into a higher *caste*, which he may hope to do if he keeps his caste law and lives a good life. On the other hand, if he lives a bad life he may well be reborn as a pig or even a worm.

Caste is the Indian class system. It dates back thousands of years and no one is quite sure how it began. What caste you belong to is the most important single fact in your life. It determines the work you do, the clothes you wear, the food you eat, the person you marry, and the treatment you get from your fellow men. Moreover, you are born into your parents' caste and throughout your life cannot change it.

The highest caste of all is the *Brahman*. A young Brahman from birth has every privilege. He has a *guru*, or teacher, to instruct him in the Scriptures, and the rules of his caste. Between the ages of eight and twelve, after an elaborate ceremony before a sacrificial fire, he is presented with the Sacred Thread, which he wears around his neck and which marks him off with other high-caste groups as "twice born" and superior to men of other castes.

At the other end of the scale is the lowest of the low, the *Outcaste* or *Untouchable*. He is a communal slave living apart from the other villagers. He has to look after the sanitation of the village, remove and skin dead animals, and generally do all the work that no one else will touch. For this he gets just enough food to keep body and soul together. If there is a famine, he is the first to die. Gandhi, the Father of Modern India, declared:

> If I have to be reborn, I would wish to be born an Untouchable, so that I might share their sorrows, their sufferings and the affronts levelled at them, in order that I might endeavor to free myself and them from this miserable condition.

India's god has 350,000 faces. So, at least, believe the wise men of Hinduism. Ninety percent of India's people live in villages and most of them are poor and uneducated. For them the idea of a universal spirit is not enough; in their religious life they must have something physical that they can see and handle. So everywhere in India there are idols representing thousands of different gods. Yet in one sense they are all Brahman, for he created them, we are told, to help people gradually to learn the truth about him.

By the roadside, in the home, and in the Hindu temple we find these images. In almost every home there is a small place reserved for the household god to whom prayers and offerings are made every day. In the temples they are huge, painted figures treated by the priests like princes: wakened to the sound of music, washed, fed, clothed, adorned with flowers, prayed to, and even on occasion taken for rides.

At Puri on the Bay of Bengal is the shrine of "The Lord of the World," Jagannatha, from which we get the English word *Juggernaut*. Every year, at the end of June, thousands of Hindus watch the triumphal procession of this huge image from his temple to a garden house a mile away. It takes two thousand men to pull his chariot. Jagannatha is very popular because he recognizes no caste distinctions.

Of all India's thousands of deities only a few are known throughout the country. The most famous are Brahma, the Creator, Vishnu, the Preserver, and Shiva, the Destroyer. Shiva also is worshiped as the creator of new life, and his symbol is a fertility stone.

Two incarnations of Vishnu are very popular, Krishna and Rama, and the Hindu Scriptures contain many stories of their exploits. Every Hindu child knows the amazing adventures of Krishna in his chariot, and the story of how Rama with the help of the monkey god, Hanuman, recovered his wife from Ceylon where a demon had hidden her.

In a very beautiful poem, known as "The Gita" or "The Song of the Lord," Krishna offers himself as a personal savior to those who will follow him. He is to be their only Lord, and by faith and meditation they may find salvation in him after death.

Thus a Hindu may worship one god alone or many gods. On the other hand, with or without the help of lesser gods, he may seek release from this world by meditation on the one all-pervading spirit, Brahman.

Hinduism, therefore, as a religion is very tolerant. It is not what a man believes that makes him a Hindu. If he is born into a caste, he is a Hindu whatever he believes.

Not only the gods are holy in India: there are, for example, seven sacred rivers. The most famous of them is the Ganges, and the most sacred city in India is on its banks—Benares, now called Varanasi. A million pilgrims visit it every year. It has 1,500 temples. Along the waterfront there are broad steps, or *ghats*, leading down to the river. They are worn by the feet of millions of pilgrims who for centuries have used them to go down to bathe in the sacred waters of the river. The pilgrims plunge beneath the surface, even gargling the water, so that every part of their bodies is purified and they can die in peace.

Lying on the ghats are the bodies of the dead, each covered with a pall and fastened securely to a bier. They remain there until the great pyres are lit each day on which they are cremated. Years ago, when a high-caste Hindu died, it was expected that his wife would throw herself into the raging flames and perish with his body. In doing this she was promised as many years future happiness with him as there are hairs on the human body.

Cows are also sacred. Millions of them wander over the countryside and through the towns. You may come across one sprawling in the shade against a building, quietly chewing its cud, or wandering into a main thoroughfare and sitting down in the path of oncoming traffic. Whoever persuades it to move on will do so gently and with reverence.

In India, Sunday is not a day of rest, and for the village people there are no yearly vacations. Instead there are many happy festival days in the year.

16

Dewali, for instance, is the New Year Festival at the end of October. On the night of the new moon everybody comes out of doors with a small lamp, and soon the whole village is twinkling with a myriad of little lights. New clothes are worn and there is much feasting and dancing.

Holi, the Springtime Festival, at the end of February, can be very boisterous. The men, dressed specially for the occasion, paint their own faces and then empty buckets of dye over their friends and neighbors if they can catch them. You can well imagine the state of the village street the next morning!

But most of the year consists neither of festivals nor pilgrimages, and a Hindu's faith is for the common tasks of life. He begins the day with a prayer from the Scriptures:

> *Let us meditate upon the most*
> *excellent light of the Creator.*
> *May he guide our minds.*

This is followed by a simple ritual and prayers before the image of his god. Again at noon and also in the evening he will repeat this act of worship, saying the name of god many times to help meditation and reciting prayers from the Scriptures. By this discipline he seeks to bring himself into harmony with the Eternal Spirit and to acquire the virtues of self-control, non-violence, truthfulness, charity, compassion for all living creatures, and above all the power to withdraw the mind from worldly affairs.

In 1947 India became independent after 150 years of British rule. Many Moslems in India then left the country and settled in the new state of Pakistan. There were terrible clashes as Hindus and Sikhs left Pakistan and Moslems from all over India tried to reach it. More than a million, it is believed, died from bloodshed, hunger, and disease. There are still, however, some 50 million Moslems left in India itself, and relations between them and the Hindus are now better.

After independence, the republican government of India declared its new constitution. This provided for all its subjects:

Justice—social, economic and political;
Liberty of thought, expression, belief, faith and worship;
Equality of status and opportunity.

This, of course, means revolution, if only a peaceful one, for all these ideals are in conflict with the caste system. To change completely the way of life and thought of a nation established over thousands of years is a stupendous task. How far are the Indians succeeding?

In the first place, Untouchability has been abolished. The outcastes are now known as the Scheduled Castes and they have their own representatives in Parliament. This is the beginning of a change of attitude which will take many years, if not centuries, to spread through the whole of India.

Another important reform is the new status of women. Under the old law of Manu, a woman was the inferior partner in any marriage. Her chief purpose was to serve her husband and if he should die before her, her usefulness in life was over. Today, all that has changed. Women are now educated, given the right to have property of their own and to enter the professions side by side with the men. In fact, India was one of the first countries in the world to have a woman prime minister.

Mahatma Gandhi was probably the greatest reformer that India has ever known. At the age of nineteen he went to London to learn to be a lawyer. He then spent twenty-one years in South Africa fighting for the rights of Indian settlers, who were badly treated there. The remainder of his life he gave to India, working for political independence and to improve the lot of the outcastes, women, and all who were downtrodden.

He lived very simply. When he went to England he promised his mother never to eat meat, take alcohol, or smoke. He kept that promise all his life. He dressed like a peasant, weaving his own clothes, and he believed that the simple village life of India was ideal. He disliked the industrial life of the Western world. He was a very devout man. "I am a Moslem, a Sikh, a Christian, and a Jew," he once said. On January 30, 1948, on his way to prayer, he was murdered by a Hindu fanatic.

He once gave his followers a rule of life:

> *I shall not fear anyone on earth; I shall fear only God. I shall not bear ill-will towards anyone; I shall not submit to injustice from anyone. I shall conquer untruth by truth and resisting untruth I shall put up with all suffering.*

Gandhi perhaps points the way for the Hinduism of tomorrow: not to drive men into the jungle to escape life but into the cities to face the stupendous problems of the new Indian republic.

BUDDHISM 2

All that we are is the result of what we have thought;
it is founded on our thoughts; it is made up of our thoughts.
If a man speaks or acts with an evil thought, pain follows him.
A tamed mind brings happiness.

Dhammapada

On June 11, 1963, a yellow-robed monk sat down in a public square in Saigon, poured gasoline over himself, lit it, and burned to death. This was the first of a number of such martyrdoms. The monks ranged in age from 17 to 73.

How can any man do this? How can he deliberately burn himself to death without flinching? We shall find the answer in our study of Buddhism.

It began in the sixth century B.C. when a young prince, named Gautama, suddenly exchanged a life of luxury for that of a penniless beggar.

His father was a wealthy Hindu who owned a vast estate a hundred miles north of Benares. He had, in fact, three palaces, one for the cold season, another for the hot season, and a third for the rainy season. When Gautama was born, it was prophesied that he would become a holy man, but his father was determined to prove the prophecy false. So he surrounded his son with every luxury, satisfied his least whim, and shielded him from the sight of anything painful. Finally, he provided him with a most beautiful wife.

But all was not well. Gautama was unhappy, and when his own son was born he called him Rahula, meaning "the fetter." Usually, when Gautama went out in his carriage, his father had the road cleared of any unpleasant sight in advance. One day, however, he drove out without his father's knowledge. On that fateful journey he saw three frightening objects: a sick man, an old man, and a dead man. Never before had he set eyes on suffering or death, but his coachman assured him that this happened to everyone.

Now Gautama, a Hindu, believed in reincarnation—an unending sequence of lives upon this earth. To face sickness, old age, and death once might be bearable but to imagine it happening to him a thousand times in the future was not to be endured. *"Surely,"* he mused, *"there must be a way of avoiding this, and I must find it."* Then he met a holy man who convinced him that by leaving home and joining other holy men he would learn how to escape from earthly life forever.

So one night, without kissing his wife and child good-bye, lest he should wake them, he crept out of the palace and with his servant rode away. At dawn he dismounted by a stream, cut off his hair, gave his sword, jewels, and his horse to his servant, and went on alone. There remained but one more thing to do. He met a beggar and exchanged his costly clothes for the beggar's rags. Now the last link with his old life was broken, and he wandered off in search of someone who could teach him a sure way of breaking the terrible cycle of reincarnation.

For a time he lived with some Brahmans, but he found their teaching useless. Then he tried Yoga and nearly died of starvation. At last he sat down under a pipal tree where he meditated alone. After forty-nine days he had a vision of all past lives and at the same moment he realized the way to release from earthly life. But on the threshold of release he halted. *"I must not do this,"* he thought. *"I must live out my life on earth, teaching all men the Way of Deliverance which I have discovered."*

Ever since that day Buddhists have looked upon this spot, Gaya, where Gautama received his enlightenment as the center of the world, and it has become a permanent Buddhist shrine.

Gautama found his way to Benares and there, in the famous Deer Park, preached his first sermon. For forty-five years he traveled, making thousands of converts by his preaching. People hailed him as "The Buddha," which means "The Enlightened One." When he died, his body was cremated and his ashes were divided and sent to the various provinces where he had preached. Other relics of his earthly body, such as teeth and hair, are said to be preserved in monuments called *stupas* in various parts of the Buddhist world.

Buddha described his teaching as **"The Middle Way of Deliverance."** He had tried the luxury of palace life and the hardships of Yoga. Both were useless to him. Salvation, he found, lay between these two extremes. While meditating under the pipal tree he discovered four important facts about life. They are called **"The Four Noble Truths."** The first three, as you may realize, are based on Hindu teaching, but the fourth is original to Buddha.

1. The Fact of Suffering

Earthly life is evil because it is full of suffering. We suffer when we are born and when we die and throughout all the years between. Even the pleasures of life are spoiled by pain and by the thought that they are soon over. We are always craving either for something that we have not got or to be rid of something that we have. Thus the sum of earthly life is misery.

2. The Cause of Suffering

The cause of all suffering is our constant craving for life to be different from what it is.

3. The End of Suffering

It follows, therefore, that once we cease to desire anything at all we cease to suffer. This is the goal of Buddhism—*Nirvana,* which means, literally, *"a blowing-out,"* the extinguishing forever of the flame of desire.

Nirvana is sometimes described as a state of joy and peace, but, in fact, it is so completely different from anything we know that it cannot be described at all.

4. The Escape from Suffering

In order to achieve Nirvana, Gautama devised **"The Noble Eightfold Path of Deliverance."** It is a course of rigorous self-discipline comprising *right beliefs, right aims, right speech, right conduct, right employment, right effort, right thinking, and right meditation.* The first two, beliefs and aims, are concerned with accepting the Buddha's teaching. The next three have to do with morals, which we shall refer to later. But the most important are the last three—effort, thought, and meditation—because they offer a sure path to Nirvana. Anyone who sought release from reincarnation in this life had to give his whole mind to them. So while Buddha laid down rules of conduct for ordinary people (laymen), he also founded an order of monks. These were men who gave up their normal way of life and devoted their whole time to the Way of Deliverance.

Discipline was very severe. Here, for example, are six of the rules Buddha gave them.

> To dress in rags.
> To wear a yellow cloak over their rags.
> To eat only once a day.
> Not to handle money.
> To possess nothing except what was given to them in their begging bowls.
> To live part of the year in the forest with only a tree for shelter and to sit on a carpet when sleeping. (To lie down was forbidden.)

A Buddhist monk got his rags from the village rubbish heap and his food from begging. It was a strict rule to eat every piece of food that was given to him. Buddha declared that the sight of his first meal made him feel very sick but he swallowed it. After that the practice became easier.

Monks had also to avoid all contact with women. *"Do not look at them, do not speak to them,"* warned Buddha. Even natural family affection had to be restrained.

Today the rules are not quite so harsh. Monks live in monasteries instead of the open air. They are allowed to own three robes, a loincloth, a begging bowl, a water filter, a razor, and a

needle. But they still spend long hours in meditation and develop remarkable powers of self-control. They believe they can, for instance, completely detach themselves from any pain their bodies suffer, as did the monks who perished in Saigon. Once a monk has reached this stage where the body counts for nothing and he finds real life only within the mind, then he is on the threshold of Nirvana; and if he should die in this state he believes that he will never return to earth again in any physical form.

Of course, only a few people in Buddhist countries become monks. The rest—and there are 300 million of them—do not hope to gain Nirvana in this life but by good works to earn for themselves a better existence in their next life on earth. Merit can be gained in many ways: by supporting the monasteries, by providing food for the monks, by making pilgrimages to Buddhist shrines, by good deeds to their fellow men, and, of course, if they have the money, by building memorials to Buddha.

In many parts of India today you can still see carved on rocks and slabs of stone the rules that a good Buddhist should keep. These were recorded by order of King Asoka, who lived 250 years before Christ. He had been a great warrior ruling most of northern India. Then one day he thought of all the suffering his conquests had caused, and he was filled with remorse. He met some Buddhist monks and was converted. The rest of his life he devoted to good works, building monasteries, roads, bridges, irrigating the land and providing for the sick and the poor. He was a delightful man to meet. He made the humblest visitor feel important and considered it an insult to keep anyone waiting who had an appointment with him. It was due to the missionaries he sent out that Buddhism became an international religion.

Many boys from Buddhist families in Southern Asia spend some weeks in a monastery when they are very young. To mark the occasion, they are first dressed in beautiful and costly robes to remind them of Gautama as a prince. Then these are stripped off them, their heads are shaved, and they don the yellow robe of the penniless monk. In the monasteries they are taught the

Buddhist Scriptures, the art of quiet meditation, and the moral rules that Buddha laid down in the Eightfold Path.

They learn that a Buddhist is truthful, that he hates lying and tale-telling. He must not boast or chatter aimlessly but speak gently and only when he has something worth saying. He must recognize evil as evil and not try to excuse himself when he has done wrong. He must not kill any living thing. Even to break an egg is forbidden. He must be honest. *"Do not take that which is not given."* He must not take intoxicants or drugs. And above all he must learn to control his thinking, for *"all that we are is the result of what we have thought."*

Everywhere in Buddhist countries there are statues of the Buddha to remind people of their faith. He is usually represented seated, with close-cropped hair, and with long lobes to his ears. His eyes may be closed, and the quiet, contented expression on his face is an invitation to meditate. One of the largest figures of Buddha is in Kamakura in Japan. It is made of bronze, forty-two feet high, and weighs one hundred and three tons.

The *pagoda* or temple is another aid to meditation. People are not generally allowed inside it, for it may contain sacred relics. But in the courtyard there are small shrines to Buddha which help the Buddhist to concentrate upon the teachings of *"The Enlightened One"* and to resolve to live a better life himself.

One of the finest Buddhist pagodas in the world, the Shwe Dagon, is in Rangoon. Its golden spires, which rise higher than a 36-story apartment building, are covered with gold leaf. It is constantly being renewed by Buddhists, who believe that by giving gold leaf to the Temple they gain merit for their next life. If they cannot afford to buy gold leaf, they can always help to sweep out the courtyards.

Is it correct to pray to Buddha? That depends on where you live. People in Southern Asia, **Theravada** Buddhists, believe that Buddha said that a man must rely entirely on himself for salvation. When Buddha died he entered Nirvana and lost all touch with this world. To pray to him would be wrong and useless.

The Buddhists in the North, **Mahavana** Buddhists, in China, Tibet, and Japan, argue that since Gautama gave up Nirvana in his lifetime in order to teach and help people, he would not forsake mankind after his death. So his spirit lives on to help those who seek it.

In these countries Buddhism, as it spread, got mixed up with the local religions. When the inhabitants said to the missionaries, "We have very excellent gods of our own," the Buddhists replied, "Oh yes, we agree, and your gods are very like Buddha." So the local gods began to be thought of as Buddhas or *Bodhisattvas* (near-Buddhas), and in northern Asia there are many Buddhas, near-Buddhas, and other divine beings.

There is, for example, Amida Buddha (the Buddha of Infinite Light), who offers a paradise called The Pure Land to those who revere him and are repeating his name silently all their working hours in case death should catch them unawares. Some use a rosary of 108 beads, passing one bead through their fingers each time they say the divine name. Also inhabiting The Pure Land is a famous Chinese goddess of mercy, Kuan Yin.

The Dalai Lama of Tibet is said to be a reincarnation of Kuan Yin. Before the Communists overran his country in 1959 he lived in a huge palace built on a rock in Lhasa, the capital of Tibet. Buried in this palace over the centuries are the remains of the previous Dalai Lamas, and it is filled with the treasures they received as gifts from other Buddhist countries.

Lama religion, as it is called, is a mixture of Buddhism and the ancient religion of Tibet called Bon. One-third of the men in Tibet used to be monks. The Drepung monastery alone was said to house 10,000 of them. Prayer wheels and prayer flags, incantations, and ritual dances in grotesque masks were an important part of Tibetan religion. Visitors to Tibet before the Communists came were rare—most of the country is 12,000 feet above sea level—but those who have met the Tibetans describe them as happy and carefree, living much of the year out-of-doors in tents, fishing on their river banks and enjoying the festivals of their religion. The Dalai Lama managed to escape from Tibet into India when the Communists occupied Tibet, and he is still regarded by his people as their spiritual leader.

A good box on the ear or a hearty peal of laughter may bring sudden enlightenment, say the **Zen** Buddhists of Japan. Reasoning, they believe, can teach us nothing about the real truth; a sudden shock may do so following an arduous course of meditation.

In a Zen monastery monks are not allowed any leisure time at all. When they are not strenuously at work in the fields or in the monastery, they are meditating. They sit in two lines facing each other, on low platforms ranged along both sides of a great hall. Cross-legged, with eyes half-closed, they meditate for many hours together. A novice master carrying a stick is often present, and if one of the monks begins to doze he is given a hearty whack.

The purpose of this meditation is to pierce the veil of thought and discover the true self that lies behind it. But first the pupil must realize the uselessness of reasoning in seeking the truth. Many techniques are employed. One, for example, is to consider insoluble problems known as *Koans*. Here is one. A man kept a goose in a bottle. The goose grew and became too big for the bottle. The man wanted to release the goose but did not wish to break the bottle. What should he do? Another technique consists of a rapid succession of questions and answers that become increasingly meaningless so that the pupil is left completely baffled.

By such means the monk reaches his limits of mental endurance, and, breaking down completely, may suddenly see himself as he really is and thus achieve his goal, enlightenment. But usually it is a long and arduous struggle. *"Only if you want enlightenment,"* declared a master Zen, *"as much as a man whose head is held under water wants air, will you get it."*

Zen has had a great influence on the Japanese way of life. Its stern discipline and rhythmic simplicity have affected many fields of activity such as painting, drama, fencing, achery, and swordsmanship. Zen is also associated with the famous Japanese tea ceremony. This is a quiet ritual carried out in the home where during the drinking of tea the family withdraws from the pressures of daily life and spends some time in quietness and meditation.

Many books have been written about Zen, and teachers of Zen are to be found today in most Western countries.

In other parts of the Buddhist world monks live quite differently from those we have just been studying. In northern Asia, for example, they are rather like parish priests in the work they do. They marry, wear black *kimonos* and silk robes, and work in the fields.

Though we find it hard to accept some forms of Buddhism, there is much it can teach us about high moral living and control of the mind.

"Look at evil as evil," said the Buddha, "and seeing evil as evil, be disgusted therewith, be cleansed of it, be freed of it." This is sound common sense as well as good morals.

"A tamed mind brings happiness" reminds us of the importance of controlling our thinking. Your aching tooth, a Buddhist would tell you, is not part of your real self. Therefore refuse to think about it, and it will lose its power over you.

There are many Buddhist groups and societies in Europe. Some Buddhists believe that Christianity is responsible for the terrible wars of this century. They send missionaries to Western countries to convert people to Buddhism, which emphasizes a nonviolent approach to life.

CONFUCIANISM 3

There is in China a famous grave nearly 2,500 years old. It lies in peaceful splendor on the river bank at Chifou, in the ancient province of Shantung, and contains the remains of one of the greatest Chinese who ever lived, Confucius.

For over twenty centuries he was the uncrowned emperor of China, for though he lived in the sixth century B.C. his teaching governed the life of China until the beginning of the present century.

After twenty-five years of Communism, the government of China ordered his grave to be renovated and Mao Tse-tung advised his party leaders to read the teaching of Confucius again.

Yet Confucius' life was in sad contrast to his later popularity. He grew up an orphan without the love of either parent; he married at nineteen, but his wife ran away from him; his son disappointed him because he did not inherit his father's brains; and the rulers of China rejected his advice and refused to put his teaching into practice.

"Alas, heaven is destroying me! Heaven is destroying me!" he cried on one occasion, overwhelmed with sadness. And at the close of his life he declared, *"No intelligent ruler arises to take me as his master. My time has come to die."*

He had one passion in life—to save his country, which was in a state of anarchy. The once mighty emperor, *The Son of Heaven*, was powerless, and in the provinces the nobles fought over the countryside, destroying homes and crops, mutilating and killing the common people. Confucius' own province was invaded twenty-one times in two hundred years.

Yet the Chinese were a brilliant people. Centuries before civilization reached the West, China had her walled cities and beautiful buildings. Architects, mathematicians, scientists, philosophers—all flourished in those days. The heavens were mapped out, sunspots observed, Halley's comet noted, the year estimated at 365¼ days, waterclocks invented (dividing each day into a hundred parts). Even the theory of evolution was expounded nearly 3,000 years before it dawned upon Europe.

How could Confucius save China? Revolution was impossible; the country was too vast. He decided to train ministers of state. He attracted young men to him and taught them how to govern properly, in the hope that lazy and incompetent nobles would employ them. After his death his teaching was recognized as immensely important, and nearly everyone appointed to public office had first to prove his training in Confucian principles. Hundreds of his sayings about life and government have been preserved and are well worth reading. Here are some of his basic beliefs.

He believed that one thing alone could save mankind—education. All men, he thought, were gentlemen by nature; it was only ignorance that made them evil. Teach man what is good and he will live a noble life. Education, therefore, must be universal.

It follows that the teacher is the most important member of the community, more important than the parent. Parents give us the life of the body, but teachers give us the life of the mind.

In China this view was rigorously held. At court, for example, everyone bowed reverently before the emperor, everyone except his tutor, who stood proudly erect while the emperor himself bowed submissively at his feet.

Only the rich were educated in Confucius' day. Music, ritual, archery, carriage driving, writing, and mathematics were the popular subjects. But for Confucius education was a far more serious business: it was training in the art of living that failed completely unless it produced the desire to love and serve one's fellowmen. *"Virtue is to love men; wisdom is to understand men,"* he said.

He required this high standard from his pupils. At his first interview a pupil would be asked politely to sit down and talk about his reasons for wanting education. Did he want to make money out of it or to impress friends? Confucius would listen intently. *"No man can hide his character,"* he said. *"Look closely at his aims, observe the means by which he pursues them, and discover what brings him content."*

Once you were accepted by him he would require the most rigorous self-discipline. No man is fit to control others, he believed, until he can control himself. At all times a pupil must be on his guard, for character is formed more when we are alone than when we are in company.

He could be quite merciless. It was his habit to criticize pupils to their faces and praise them behind their backs. They must never lose their tempers. They were to be fearless in speech but always polite, especially at home and to the elderly. He despised the man who was servile to those above him and bullying towards those beneath him.

He was impatient with lazy people. *"I won't teach a man,* he declared, *"who is not trying to make things clear to himself. If I explain one-fourth and the man does not go away and think out the remaining three-fourths for himself, I won't bother to teach him."*

Confucius distrusted clever talkers and warned his pupils that they were dangerous. His pupils were to be careful in speech, never talking except when they had something worth saying. But they should be resolute in action. First they must think out properly what they intended to do and count the cost of it. Then, having set on a course of action, they must carry it through.

The truly educated man was always humble. *"Do not be concerned,"* he said, *"because you are not in office, but with making yourself qualified for office; do not be concerned that you are unknown, but with being worthy of reputation."*

He knew nothing of democracy. He taught obedience. The son should obey his father and respect his elder brothers. The father should obey the ruler, though bad rulers should not be tolerated.

He had great respect for the wisdom of old age. He believed that those at the end of life had much to teach those at the beginning.

Confucius taught nothing about God. He did, however, refer to himself as being sent by Heaven and he added many improvements to the religious ceremonies of his day, which were mainly concerned with ancestor worship. All men were brothers, and he thought strife between nations was stupid. He taught the negative form of the golden rule: *"What you do not wish others to do to you, do not unto them."*

Usually he was a happy man. He loved to play the lute, to fish and to drive a carriage. He believed music and poetry should play a big part in education and later life. He was courageous. When his followers were frightened by some passing danger, he would sit down by the roadside, play his lute and sing songs until their fear had gone. He was humble. *"I never walk with two companions,"* he declared, *"but I learn something."*

His teaching produced very successful rulers for many centuries and he did more than anyone else to form the Chinese character. Through him, for example, the Chinese gained the reputation of being the most polite nation on earth.

TAO   4

Flower children, Beautiful People, Hippies, Love Movement, New Society—these are some of the names by which young people who in recent years opted out of society have described themselves. Disgusted by the way older people were running the world, they formed groups of their own, adopted different styles of dress, music, and speech, issued newspapers, records, and posters, all of which expressed a new attitude to life. By various striking experiments of "freak-outs" with sound, color, light, movement, and drugs they sought what they called psychedelic experience—an expanding of the mind to receive new and disturbing sensations. And by "read-ins" and "think-ins" they sought a new way of life on a peaceful and happy basis.

Nearly every generation produces some kind of protest movement. This generation's rebellion may seem revolutionary, but its cause has much in common with one that took place in China just over two thousand years ago.

China had passed through centuries of lawlessness. This was gradually followed by the rather severe form of government which Confucius advocated. Taoism (pronounced Dowism) was a movement first in protest against lawlessness then later against Confucian government. Taoists looked upon both as an interference with personal liberty. This protest was first expressed in the writings of a man called Lao-tzu.

Not very much is known about him. The traditional story sounds highly improbable. His real name, we are told, was Li-Uhr and he was seventy-two and white haired when he was born. He was therefore nicknamed Lao-tzu, which means Old Boy.

He worked as a librarian at the court of a local ruler, but he found court life so disgusting with its vicious struggle for power and wealth that he gave up his job and wandered off in a cart pulled by two black oxen. At the gate of the city, as he was about to leave, he wrote a short book and gave it to the porter. He was last seen high up in some neighboring mountains disappearing into a cloud.

Some scholars doubt that Lao-tzu ever existed. The book, however, exists and is entitled *The Book of the Way and Its Power*. For many centuries it had a great influence on the Chinese way of life, and together with later Tao writings still appeals to people dissatisfied with the busy, aimless world around them.

Taoism declares that behind the scenes of human life there is a universal, creative force, the Tao. Though it is not usually thought of as a god, it has personal qualities. It loves and nourishes everything, yet has no desire to meddle in human affairs or to possess anything for itself. In a quiet, motherly way it inspires the universe with peace and order. For example, if we observe the effortless sequence of the seasons we note that everything happens without fuss and commotion, and if we study the heavens we observe a similar order and harmony.

Human life also should proceed like this, and the object of the man of Tao is to share in the general harmony of nature. One translation of the word "Tao" is "The Way," and Taoism is therefore a way of life.

Men should cease to bicker and quarrel and fight over material possessions. They should rather take as an example the qualities of water. Water is gentle, acts quickly, overcomes all things, and benefits all men. Yet it always seeks the lowest place. So man should design his life: orderly and unhurried, humble and controlled, ambitious only to benefit mankind.

To the man of Tao there is only one way to settle disputes—by discussion. Human warfare is unnatural; the man of Tao hates the sight of weapons. He respects all life, human, animal, and insect. He returns good for evil. He is simple and modest in his way of life and interferes only to relieve others of their ills.

Taoism developed in ways quite unlike anything Lao-tzu had in mind. These included belief in magic, and priests who could overcome devils, sickness, drought, and other calamities by casting spells.

It also produced a distinguished teacher in the fourth century B.C. called Chuang-tzu. He was a mystic. One day he fell asleep and dreamed he was a butterfly fluttering happily from flower to flower. When he awoke, he said that he did not know whether he had been a man dreaming that he was a butterfly or whether he had been a butterfly dreaming that he was a man. In this and other ways Chuang-tzu showed his doubt about whether the world was real. This uncertainty was a further reason for penetrating the appearance of things to the reality that lay behind them.

Many young people in every age have felt, with Lao-tzu, a sense of frustration with life as they find it. They protest against the dull routine of daily life, its fuss and worry, its petty aims and meaningless restrictions. They seek liberty and would agree perhaps with Lao-Tzu when he said,

There has been such a thing as letting mankind alone.
There has never been such a thing as governing mankind.

But Lao-tzu sought liberty from the discipline of others only to impose a stricter discipline upon himself.

He who knows himself is enlightened.
He who conquers himself is mighty.

This search for inner harmony through self-control and meditation soon became popular in China. Later it spread to Japan where it inspired another great religious movement which we have already studied, Zen Buddhism.

SHINTO 5

At nine o'clock, Japanese time, on August 6, 1945, an atomic bomb exploded over Hiroshima and a second one over Nagasaki at noon on August 9.

These two horrifying attacks on Japan not only wiped out two great cities but destroyed the Japanese war effort and with it the main religion of Japan, *State Shinto*.

Shinto is a word meaning *The Way of the Gods*. It was coined by Buddhist missionaries to describe the religion they found in Japan. They discovered that the Japanese worshiped a multitude of gods and nature spirits. Today, fourteen centuries later, Shinto remains very much the same.

But State Shinto was a modern version of this ancient religion. It was based upon the belief that in the seventh century B.C. the most famous of all Japanese deities, Amaterasu, the sun goddess, married her son to the daughter of the god of Fujiyama, the great snow-capped volcano of Japan. Their grandson became the first Japanese emperor. It was believed therefore that the royal line was descended from the gods and all Japanese emperors were divine.

For many years before the Second World War the Japanese government encouraged this belief. Over 300 shrines were devoted to emperor worship. To acknowledge the divinity of the emperor was a test of loyalty that no Japanese could afford to ignore. Children in school were taught to bow to his portrait and to recite the names of 124 past emperors. Since the emperor was divine, they were told, he would one day rule the world.

To die for the emperor during the war was to become a god oneself. Many Japanese airmen eagerly hurled themselves as well as their bombs at the enemy targets, and many soldiers committed *hara-kiri* rather than fall into enemy hands.

Despite this fanatical devotion, the Japanese lost the war. On December 31, 1945, the Emperor Hirohito declared to his people that he was not divine and the idea that the Japanese were superior to all other races and would rule the world was completely false. So State Shinto died.

For a long time after this the Japanese seemed to lose faith in religion, but gradually they returned to their ancient worship of many gods as well as to Buddhism.

So everywhere in Japan we find shrines, from the smallest— the god-shelf in the home where household gods and ancestors are revered—to the largest, such as the famous one to the sun goddess at Ise which covers many square miles of parkland.

Even a stranger to Shinto cannot fail to be impressed by the beauty and peace that surround these sacred places. The worshiper first passes under a wooden archway known as a *torii*. He is now on holy ground and washes his hands in the water provided, as an act of purification. Next, he comes upon a hall, a large building consisting mainly of pillars, which is used on occasions for special rituals, dances, pantomimes, and other religious entertainments, for Japan is a country of many festivals. Finally he reaches the shrine itself, usually a one-story building approached up a number of broad steps.

He does not enter the shrine, for sacred relics are kept within. He rings a bell to inform the god of his presence, recites some verses, says a prayer, and makes an offering of money or rice before leaving. In recent years the priests who look after the shrines have encouraged families to bring their young children to the shrines for blessing and later to have them married there.

There is another form of Shinto in Japan that provides for congregational worship, *Sect Shinto*. There are many sects in Japan, and like Buddhism and Christianity they offer the opportunity of belonging to a religious community. These congregations meet regularly to worship a particular god or to study

42

beliefs that may come from Buddha, Confucius, or their own founder. One of the largest sects in Japan holds beliefs very similar to Christian Science. It has ten thousand temples and about ten million members.

Other religions exist in Japan side by side with Shinto, and nothing prevents a good Shintoist from following them too. As a baby he may be blessed at a Shinto shrine, as a man follow the teaching of Confucius, and when he dies he may be cremated by a Buddhist priest.

JUDAISM   6

"Israeli tanks reach the Suez Canal."

Twice in recent years this headline has startled the world. In 1967 the Israelis defeated their Arab neighbors with lightning speed and threatened to destroy them. Again in 1974 the Israelis and Arabs fought, with an uneasy truce finally being reached under UN auspices. In all this fighting the Israelis had no intention of destroying the Arabs. All they sought was to keep their own little territory of Israel safe. It was given to them in May 1948, and because they feel that every square foot is precious they have slaved from the beginning to make it fertile and prosperous. Establishing Kibbutzim, or farm settlements, they fought rocks, sand, and drought until, to quote their Scriptures, they made *"the desert to blossom as the rose."*

Why then do they have to fight their neighbors? Look for a moment at a map. All around Israel are Arab countries. When Israel was established in Palestine by the United Nations at the end of the Second World War, thousands of Arabs left the area, though today 300,000 live in Israel, enjoying equal rights of citizenship with the Israelis. But those who left were never absorbed by the surrounding nations. In the Gaza Strip, poverty-stricken and neglected, they became a living reproach and a constant reminder to the Arabs that, right in the middle of their world, they had what was to them a country which had no right to exist, Israel.

The Israelis take a different view! For them the Arabs are the usurpers. Not merely for twenty years but for 4,000 years Palestine has been the Jewish homeland. Abraham, the father of the race, arrived there over 1,900 years before Christ was born. There he established the Hebrew nation, the forefathers of the Jews, and ever since they have been struggling to remain there. Look at this list of their misfortunes.

20th century B.C.		Established in Palestine
17th(?) " "		To Egypt and slavery
13th " "		**Return To Palestine**
12th " "		Invaded by the Philistines
8th " "		Deported to Assyria
6th " "		Deported to Babylon
6th " "		**Return To Palestine**
4th " "		Conquered by Alexander the Great
4th " "		Annexed by one of his generals
2nd " "		Independence rewon
1st century A.D.		Occupied by the Romans
1st " "		Temple at Jerusalem destroyed
2nd " "		Banished by the Romans
20th " "		**Return To Palestine**

Down the long centuries everyone seemed to covet their country. Philistines, Egyptians, Assyrians, Babylonians, Persians, Greeks, Romans, and Arabs battered and bullied them, massacred and deported them, and for most of the time denied them the right to live there.

Yet this is only part of the story of their sufferings. Through most of the eighteen centuries when they were scattered abroad, they were the outcasts of humanity. Hitler's brutal massacre of six million Jewish men, women, and children was only one episode in this story of man's inhumanity to man. The early Christian Church tried to convert them and, failing to do so, persecuted them. The new religion, Islam, in the seventh century followed suit. The rabble that followed the Crusades believed that to kill a Jew would save a Christian from purgatory. In 1290 the Jews were expelled from England to the accompaniment of howling, violent mobs. Between 1348 and 1350 the entire Jewish population of Germany was almost wiped out. In 1492 they were expelled from Spain. In 1495 they were ordered to leave Portugal but to leave behind all their children under fourteen to be brought up as Christians. Natural calamities were blamed upon them: when plague broke out thousands were roasted alive. And for their faith they suffered the most appalling horrors at the hands of the Inquisition.

Not until the eighteenth century did conditions greatly improve for them. And only in 1858 were British Jews allowed to become members of Parliament and in 1871 to take degrees at Oxford and Cambridge.

Though there is much less anti-Semitism today, it occasionally flares up, particularly in the Near East. Only education and democracy will finally close this disgraceful chapter in man's history.

The Wailing Wall is the most sacred spot in Jerusalem. After their recent victories the Jews crowded to it, and whenever they have been allowed to do so, they have said their prayers there. The distant sound of their praying has given the wall its nickname. It is part of the ancient wall that used to surround the Temple of King Solomon.

Now there is no Temple; the *synagogue* is the meeting place for worship. The most important day of the week is Saturday, for the Jewish *Sabbath* begins at sunset on Friday and finishes twenty-four hours later.

The second of the Ten Commandments says, *"You shall not make for yourself a graven image."* Inside a synagogue, therefore, there are no pictures, images, statues, or representations of any person, lest this should tend towards idolatry.

The people in the congregation sit facing Jerusalem, and in front of them, hidden by a curtain, is a chest called *the Ark of the Covenant*. Before it hangs a small lamp which is never allowed to go out. Within the ark are kept scrolls of the Law (*the Tora*), which Christians know as the Pentateuch. During some of the synagogue services the Torah is carried around the synagogue; everybody present turns toward it and either bows or touches it as a mark of respect. Men and women usually sit separately, and the men all wear a head covering—a hat or skull cap—in addition to a prayer shawl called a *talet*.

At the age of thirteen a boy is prepared for adult membership in the synagogue. It is an exciting occasion when he is received and, standing before the congregation, reads from the Scriptures in Hebrew. Men are essential for the life of the synagogue, for a service cannot be held unless ten males over the age of thirteen are present.

To the Jew, home is as important as the synagogue. On the doorpost at the entrance you may see a small cylinder or box. This is called a *Mezuzah*. It contains fifteen verses of Scripture minutely printed on a scroll. On entering the house a Jew will touch it with his finger, reminding himself that a Jewish home, like a synagogue, is a sacred place. In it many religious ceremonies are observed. These responsibilities are left to the Jewish woman, whose religious duties in the house are of comparable importance to those of the man in the synagogue.

The *Talmud*, a special book of instructions, declares, *"He who has no wife lives without happiness, without religion, and without blessing."* To every practicing Jew it is an important part of his religious duty to marry and bring up a family. In a Jewish marriage ceremony the bride and bridegroom sip wine together to signify that they will share the burden of all that life brings them. And in honoring their marriage vows, in their devotion to their children and their old people, Jewish families set an example to the world.

One day in 1947 an Arab goatherd, Muhammad the Wolf, was seeking some stray goats along the shores of the Dead Sea in Palestine. He threw a stone into a cave and heard a sound like breaking pottery. Rather scared, he ran away but came back later to investigate with a companion. In the cave they found many jars containing strange objects wrapped in linen and covered with pitch. These were the first of the famous *Dead Sea Scrolls* of which many others have since been found in the neighborhood.

Among these scrolls are some of the books of the Old Testament written in Hebrew 1,900 years ago. Before this discovery the earliest copies known were written in the ninth century A.D. In the 800 years between the two sets of manuscripts, over twenty generations of Jews had copied and recopied these Old Testament books. Yet only the slightest differences are to be found between the earlier and the later versions. This shows the infinite care the Jews have taken to preserve the accuracy of their Scriptures. In times of persecution again and again they have rescued the scrolls before their synagogues have been ransacked or burned down.

With the same care they preserve their ancient customs. When they lived in Palestine there were each year pilgrimages to the Temple, for *Passover* at the barley harvest, for *Pentecost* at the wheat harvest and for *Tabernacles* at the fruit harvest. Today, without a Temple, they keep the festivals with all their ancient ritual, in the setting of their own homes.

"Why is this night different from all other nights?" asks the youngest child in the family on the eve of the Passover. Then his father explains how this festival recalls a night 3,000 years ago when their ancestors were slaves in Egypt, when, during the hours of darkness, the Angel of Death passed over their homes to smite the Egyptians, and Moses led them hurriedly out into the desert. During the Passover meal which follows and for the next eight days, the family eats *Matzos,* unleavened bread, to remind them of their ancestors' departure from Egypt, and a nut and apple paste to remind them of the mud they used to make bricks during their slavery.

Other festivals have their dramatic moments. One especially pleasing to children is *The Feast of Lights* in December. It commemorates a great victory in 165 B.C. when the Jews freed their land from a tyrant called Antiochus Epiphanes. The festival lasts eight days, and each day a fresh candle is lit, games are often played, and children receive presents.

New Year's Day in the Jewish calendar comes in September or October. In 1969, for example, it was September 13th and began the year 5730. According to ancient tradition, this would be the number of years since the Era of Creation.

New Year's Day and the *Day of Atonement* comprise a solemn festival. It is a time of repentance, and many Jewish businesses shut down to observe the festival. During the *Day of Atonement* a twenty-five hour fast is observed. Young children try to give up one meal.

Religion is never far from the thoughts of practicing Jews. Every night and morning they will say *The Shema*, the commandments of God found in Deuteronomy 6:4-9. Every Friday evening candles are lit and prayers said before the special meal begins a new sabbath. On the sabbath, strict Jews will not travel or even use a telephone. In Israel shops shut, trains do not run, and all work is reduced to a minimum.

In captivity and exile the Jews believed that God would one day send them a great Deliverer, or Messiah, to restore their country to them. Though this idea of a personal Messiah is not held so widely today, the Jews have always believed that God in a special way would reveal himself to mankind through them, His Chosen People. We should not forget that through centuries of paganism in ancient times the Jewish altar and later the synagogue were often the only witnesses to a belief in one righteous and loving God.

It is quite impossible to estimate the influences of Judaism in the world. Jesus, the founder of Christianity, was a practicing Jew who based his teaching on the Old Testament. *"I have come,"* he declared, *"to fulfill the Law, not to destroy it."* Muhammad, the founder of Islam, was so deeply influenced by Jewish teaching that at first he wished to unite with the Jews in one religion. Hence we can say that both Christianity and Islam are daughter religions of Judaism.

And today, the Jewish Law has much to teach us. We cannot read *The Ten Commandments* (Exodus 20), for example, without feeling that the world would be a much happier and safer place if these commandments were sincerely kept by all men.

CHRISTIANITY 7

The via dolorosa was so crowded that His Holiness was unable to pause at The Stations of the Cross but was swept onwards to the Place of the Skull.

So a reporter described the wild enthusiasm which greeted Pope Paul VI when he visited Jerusalem for three days in early January 1964.

No pope previously had ever traveled by airplane; none had even left Italy since 1809 when Pius VII was compelled to go to France to crown Napoleon as emperor of the French.

The Pope lives at the Vatican in Vatican City in Rome which, with its 108.7 acres, is the smallest state in the world. He is head of the *Roman Catholic Church* which has 670 million members, 125 cardinals, 2,600 bishops and 420,000 priests.

This is the largest of the three branches of the Christian Church. The other two are known as the *Orthodox Church* and the *Protestant Church*. Together, with nearly one billion followers, they form the largest religious community in the world.

Its founder was Jesus, the humble carpenter of Nazareth. He was born about 6 B.C. and lived for just over thirty years. No more than three of these were spent in teaching. Yet in this short space of time he spoke and acted in such a way that he has had a far greater influence on the human race than anyone else who has ever lived, and after 2,000 years more people profess Christianity today than ever before.

What was there about Jesus that made him unique? It would be interesting to compare him with the founders of other religions and to try and discover the secret of his personal magnetism.

Four short books called *Gospels* describe for us a few episodes in his life. Here we have a vivid picture of a man praying in the early hours of the morning, working from dawn to dusk, teaching and healing and traveling from one town to another. He radiates joy and peace, and great crowds follow him. He delights them with his stories; he astonishes them with his miracles. He visits their homes, blesses their children, banishes their worries, shares their sorrows, heals their diseases and forgives their sins.

Everyone can understand his message. He offers a gift called *The Kingdom of Heaven,* which in fact means the rule of God in a man's life. This gift is subject to certain conditions: a man shall be thoroughly dissatisfied with his past life, he shall accept the word of Christ with simple faith, and he shall commit his life to the guidance of God. There is no need to become a monk or hermit; this is a workaday religion for ordinary people.

Jesus was very concerned about human suffering. Wherever he went, he relieved it, and he expected his followers to do the same. If they could prevent it or soften it for others, they were to do so. But what they could not alter they should accept as he accepted it. God knows perfectly well what he is doing in this world and although here we *"see through a glass darkly,"* in the next life the mystery of suffering will be explained.

Jesus was also deeply concerned about the power of sin in men's lives. He condemned the selfish and useless life and all those who inflicted suffering. *"The gate is wide that leads to Perdition,"* he said. *"There is plenty of room on the road, and many go that way."*

The ruling classes put Jesus to death. They denounced him as a fraud and a danger to established authority. It was the only way, they felt, to silence him and to save the country from revolution.

Jesus knew that this would be the end of his work and he taught his disciples that it was necessary for him to die in order that his teaching should live. *"I, if I be lifted up* (on the Cross), *will draw all men unto me,"* he declared.

In the Gospels it is recorded that Jesus performed many miracles. The greatest miracle was his own resurrection. The Gospels describe several appearances after he came out of the tomb. This amazing event has puzzled men in every generation. How could such a thing possibly happen? When Paul told the people of Athens about it, they laughed at him.

But perhaps the more interesting question is, how could it not have happened? His disciples ran away when he was arrested. They hid themselves after his crucifixion lest the same ghastly fate should befall them. Then suddenly they sprange into action, openly and fearlessly declaring that he was alive again. Was it a delusion? Most of them met with a violent end, and men do not suffer torture and death for something that they are not utterly convinced is true.

Could there have been a Christian religion without the Resurrection? Paul, the earliest and greatest missionary, did not think so. *"If Christ is not risen,"* he declared, *"then is our preaching vain."*

For a thousand years after Christ's death Christians remained united. When they met one another, there were no questions such as, "What Church do you belong to?" "What denomination are you?" For all Christians belonged to the one church that is now known as the **Roman Catholic** Church. Then in 1054 it broke in two. Christians in eastern Europe formed the **Orthodox Church.** Today it has 150 million members and its most important official is known as *the Patriarch of Constantinople.*

When the Pope visited Jerusalem in 1964, he met and embraced the Patriarch. *"This is an event,"* he declared, *"which can have great historical importance,"* for Pope and Patriarch had not met since 1439.

The Orthodox Church in some ways is similar to the Roman Catholic Church. Its buildings are ornate and its services elaborate. Some of its ceremonies are very picturesque. During the early hours of Easter Sunday, in a closely packed and darkened church, the priests make a pretense of searching for the body of Christ. Then suddenly the cry is heard, **"Christ is risen!"** Immediately everyone lights a candle and holds it aloft, and to the thunderous response, **"Christ is risen indeed!"** they celebrate the Resurrection in a blaze of light.

A solitary piece of parchment nailed to a church door on October 31, 1517, founded the third section of the Christian Church. On this parchment, Martin Luther, a priest in Wittenberg, protested against many things he felt were wrong with the Roman Catholic Church. As a result **the Protestant Church** was born, or as it is called in some countries, *the Lutheran Church*. The Church in England finally became Protestant in Queen Elizabeth's reign and has remained so ever since.

On April 20, 1953, the Archbishop of Canterbury presented a Bible to Queen Elizabeth II at her coronation. He said, *"Our gracious Queen: to keep your majesty ever mindful of the Law and the Gospel of God as the Rule for the whole life and government of Christian princes, we present you with this Book, the most valuable thing which the world affords."*

The Protestant Church teaches that a man's salvation is dependent upon his personal relationship with God and that the Bible is his sole guide to faith and conduct. So an English monarch, who is bound by law to be a Protestant, is always presented with a Bible at his or her coronation. This law was made centuries ago as a result of the unhappy struggle in England between Roman Catholics and Protestants.

Because Protestants are not bound to any one organization or priesthood, there are many different sects among them. Over two hundred are recognized in the United States alone, and in England there are many different Protestant churches, of which the largest is *the Church of England* governed by two archbishops and several bishops who are each responsible for an area called a diocese. Its services are to be found in the Church of England *Book of Common Prayer*.

In this prayer book you will also find the three creeds, or statements of belief, on which Christianity is founded. The most important is *The Apostles' Creed*, which is over 1,800 years old. The opening declaration is accepted by most Christians today:

I believe in God, the Father Almighty, maker of heaven and earth and in Jesus Christ his only Son, our Lord.

Many towns have a memorial to a man who rode a quarter of a million miles on horseback. *"The world is my parish,"* he declared. His name was John Wesley and every *Methodist* church is a tribute to his remarkable achievement. He was a Church of England clergyman who grew impatient with his own church as Martin Luther did with his. In two hundred years Methodism has spread into many parts of the world. It is one of the strongest Protestant churches in the United States.

The *Baptist Church* by its name indicates its difference from other Protestant churches. Baptists do not believe in infant baptism. Instead, adults are baptized in church as a sign of their commitment to God. For this purpose a shallow well is used which is usually built into the floor of the church in front of the pulpit.

There are other large groups of Protestants, such as *Congregationalists,* from which the Baptists came, *Presbyterians,* and *The Salvation Army.* Most of these churches suffered severe persecution in their early years.

> *"This is my body; this is my blood.*
> *Do this in remembrance of me."*

These were the words of Jesus as he broke bread and handed it with wine to his disciples on the night before he died. The most solemn service in many Christian Churches is based upon this act of Christ's, and is known by various names: the Mass, Holy Communion, the Eucharist, and the Sacrament of the Lord's Supper.

Christians keep December 25 as the anniversary of Christ's birth, Easter in remembrance of his death and resurrection, and Pentecost to celebrate the gift of the Holy Spirit.

Christianity is a missionary religion. There have been over 1,200 translations of the Bible, and every year millions of Bibles are printed and distributed around the world. During the early years of the Christian Church, despite persecution, Christianity spread throughout Europe. *"The more you mow us down,"* declared Tertullian, an early Christian writer, *"the more we grow."* In later centuries it spread throughout most of the world, so that over large areas of the earth's surface the only churches, hospitals, and schools that existed were built, staffed, and paid for by Christians. The reason for this is to be found in the Gospels. Repeatedly Jesus directed his followers to *"preach the Gospel,"* and his vivid descriptions of the Good Samaritan (Luke 10) and the Last Judgment (Matthew 25) showed them that he felt religion without care for one's neighbor was useless.

Christianity has often met with bitter opposition. In the first three hundred years of its history, Christians were continually put to death for their faith: thrown to the lions, sawn in two, crucified, or burned alive. The last Roman emperor to persecute them was Diocletian. Finding none of these penalties really effective, he devised a new one. Christians had their right eyes gouged out with a sword and the tendons of their legs cut. Nevertheless, the Church grew until Rome gave in and recognized it officially.

In the twentieth century opposition has again been fierce. Thousands of Christians died in concentration camps in Germany when they refused to accept Hitler's racial teaching. In Russia, for over fifty years, there has been antireligious teachings in all schools, and Christians together with Jews have continually suffered for their faith. But persecution has the same effect today as it had in the Roman Empire. The Russian Orthodox Church claims to have a membership about four times the size of the Russian Communist party.

No honest Christian would maintain that the Church has been perfect. In years gone by, it has persecuted as hotly as it has been persecuted and has often encouraged superstition and opposed the advance of scientific knowledge. But wherever it spread the teaching of Jesus, it brought hope and joy to those who accepted it. Often it was in the forefront of reform.

It is sometimes said, "Christianity has failed because it has never been tried." This is partly true. Read in a modern version *The Sermon on the Mount,* Matthew 5,6,7, and you will realize the very high standards of conduct Jesus expected from his followers. Few Christians in any generation have lived up to this teaching, but for all Christians it is at least an ideal on which they try to model their lives.

Today, Christians have two main objects in view. One is to forget their old differences and unite in worship and action. So Pope and Patriarch have met in Jersualem; so in London, for example, Roman Catholics and Protestants have joined at Easter in united services in St. Paul's or Westminster Cathedral. A very active *World Council of Churches* organizes united Christian action and expresses a Christian view on world affairs. Second, new methods of worship are being tried out, and a new presentation of the Gospel is being sought that will be more suitable to our present age. For Christians still believe that Christianity is the final answer to the world's problems.

ISLAM 8

Allah is most great! I bear witness that there is no god but Allah. I bear witness that Muhammad is the Apostle of Allah. Come to prayer! Prayer is better than sleep.

Every few hours for more than thirteen centuries this compelling cry has echoed over the entire Islamic, or Moslem, world. And five times a day in obedience to it, Moslems turn toward Mecca, the Holy City, unroll their prayer mats and prostrate themselves before Allah.

The prayer is always the same, one of adoration. It should be repeated seventeen times a day. At the beginning of the prayer the worshiper stands erect, his thumbs touching the lobes of his ears; at the end, by a series of movements, he is prostrate, with knees and forehead on the ground. He prays wherever he happens to be when he hears the *muezzin's,* or crier's, call. Only once a week, on Friday at noon, is he required to attend a *mosque,* the Moslem house of prayer.

Inside the mosque, the men (women do not usually attend) stand in rows facing a niche which indicates the direction of Mecca. In front of them, also facing Mecca, *the imam,* or prayer leader, begins the prostrations. Everyone follows his words and movements exactly. During the service a short address may be given from the pulpit.

The great mosques of Islam are among the most beautiful buildings in the world. In their grounds are the delicate slender towers, *minarets,* from which the call to prayer is made. There are often cloisters, pools or fountains, for worshipers are expected to wash their hands, feet, and heads before praying. Visitors are impressed by the grandeur of archways, marble domes, and rich mosaic or tile work which covers them. No one may enter a mosque without first removing his shoes.

Within the mosque he may hear a passage from the **Koran** being read. This is the sacred book of the Moslem religion. It consists of 114 chapters in the Arabic language. Children in school repeat it continually until some of them can recite the whole book. It is treated with great reverence. Within the sound of its being read no Moslem will speak, smoke, eat, or drink. For him it is the final revelation of God, given word by word to the founder of their religion, Muhammad.

Muhammad was born in Mecca about 570 A.D. Early in his life he became caravan merchant, traveling with merchandise across Arabia into the busy towns around the eastern borders of the Mediterranean. When he was twenty-five he married his employer, Khadija, who was then forty. He was very fond of her and took no other wives while she was alive.

At the age of forty he became disturbed about his religious life and began to wander over the countryside. One day in a cave he had a terrifying experience. First he saw the eyes, then the face of an unearthly being whom he later recognized as the angel Gabriel. Then in letters of fire the angel gave him this command:

> Recite in the name of your Lord, the Creator,
> Who created men from clots of blood,
> Recite! Your Lord is the Most Bounteous One
> Who by the pen has taught mankind
> Things they did not know.

Muhammad ran home in fear to be comforted by his wife.

But for twenty-three years after this Muhammad had similar experiences during which he received the teachings now preserved in the Koran. Immediately before a revelation Muhammad was usually in great mental anguish, sweat pouring from his brow. He complained of a throbbing in his brain like the heavy thud of muffled bells. This is why bells are unknown in Islam for summoning men to prayer.

Muhammad then began to declare in Mecca that there was only one god, Allah, and that he, Muhammad, was his prophet. Few people believed him. "You say you are the true prophet of Allah," jibed his opponents one day. "Then prove it by working a miracle." Muhammad replied that he had done so already: he had produced the Koran. If they did not consider that a miracle, let them compose ten verses like it!

He was very unpopular. He condemned all the idols in the town and then declared that if anyone refused his teaching and worshiped them he would go to hell. One day his cousin, who was head of his clan, came to see him. "Our grandfather worshiped idols," he said. "Is he in hell, too?" Muhammad reluctantly agreed that he must be. When the clan heard of it, they were so angry that they withdrew protection from him. Now, as an outlaw, his life was in constant danger.

Fortunately, the people of a town, Yathreb, 250 miles north of Mecca (later called Medina in his honor) invited him to be their governor. Muhammad gladly accepted, but his problem was to get there without being assassinated by the Meccans. One night he slipped out of Mecca, went some distance south, hid in a cave, and three days later took a little known route and arrived in Medina safely.

The people of Medina were so pleased to see him that he had many offers of hospitality. Unwilling to offend anyone, he remounted his camel and said, *"I will build my house wherever my camel stops."* This he did and after his death it was converted into a mosque where his body lies today.

Muhammad's journey to Medina is known as the *Hegira*, or Migration, and the year it took place, 622, became Year 1 in the Moslem calendar.

The people of Medina admired him immensely. He was a most impressive figure, powerfully built, broad across the chest and shoulders. His eyes were sharp and intelligent, his hair thick, and his black beard long and luxuriant. He spoke little and never without purpose. When annoyed, he would turn

away; when pleased, lower his eyes. Most people gladly accepted both his leadership and his new teaching.

But with Mecca he remained at loggerheads. There were many skirmishes with their caravans and occasional pitched battles in one of which Muhammad nearly lost his life and was lucky to escape with the loss of two teeth. Once he outwitted a force of 10,000 Meccans by having a deep wide trench dug in their path. Whilst arguing how to overcome this obstacle they were caught by the annual rains and had to return home, bedraggled and dispirited. But gradually through his contacts Muhammad won so many friends and admirers in Mecca that finally, after a mere show of force, they opened the city gates and let him in.

Unfortunately, within two years he was dead. Having returned to Medina, he was planning further conquests when he fell ill. After a few days of high fever he died in the arms of his favorite wife, Ayesha.

After his death Islam spread rapidly into Syria and Persia, along the north coast of Africa and into Spain, Portugal, and Southern France. With the passing of the centuries this great empire crumbled and disappeared. But the Moslem faith remained. Today there are about 400 million Moslems, living mainly in North Africa, the Middle East, Asiatic Russia, Pakistan, India, Malaysia, Bangladesh, and Indonesia.

They accept what are known as **The Five Pillars of the Faith.** The first is the faith simply expressed: *"There is no god but Allah and Muhammad is his prophet."* This is the central teaching of the Koran. Next comes the daily practice of *prayer* that has already been described. The Koran requires a minimum of three periods of prayer per day, but the usual practice is five: at daybreak, noon, mid-afternoon, after sunset, and later in the evening.

Another pillar is *almsgiving*. Muhammad instituted the first welfare state when he required all Moslems to contribute two and a half percent of their incomes to the relief of poverty and suffering. This is no secret giving, for officials are often appointed to see that no Moslem overlooks this duty.

A fourth pillar is *fasting*. For a whole month during the famous *Fast of Ramadan*, Moslems must not eat or drink between sunrise and sunset. In hot climates this can be a great hardship, and when, with the rise of the new moon it ends, there is great feasting and rejoicing.

Finally there is *pilgrimage*. For all Moslems Mecca is the holiest city on earth, so holy in fact that non-Moslems are never allowed to set foot in it. But all believers are expected to make at least one pilgrimage there in a lifetime.

In Mecca there is an ancient rectangular shrine called the Kaaba. It is said to have been built by Abraham and his son Ishmael. Embedded in one of its walls is a black stone believed to have fallen out of heaven. The Kaaba is covered with a richly embroidered tapestry that is renewed annually. Before Muhammad took Mecca, the Kaaba was full of idols. Muhammad destroyed them all.

A pilgrim must dress in two white sheets sewn together. he must not cut his hair or nails from the moment he leaves home until he begins the return journey. In Mecca he must go round the Kaaba seven times; he must stand upon a neighboring hill in meditation from noon to sunset with only an umbrella to shield him from the sun; he must also make a sacrifice.

Nowadays, as Moslems are so widely scattered over the earth's surface, those who live thousands of miles from Mecca make visits to shrines and holy places nearer to them. One famous shrine is in Jerusalem: the beautiful Dome of the Rock, covering the place from where, it is said, Muhammad made a journey to heaven.

To reach heaven—and the Koran gives vivid descriptions of both heaven and hell—the Moslem must do more than observe the Five Pillars of the Faith. He must be upright and just in all his dealings and must honor his parents. He must not drink alcohol, gamble, make idols, or possess more than four wives. As in the Jewish religion, meat must be slaughtered and prepared in a special way, and certain foods, such as pork, are prohibited altogether.

When Muhammad took Mecca and ransacked the Kaaba, he left one picture there—that of Mary and Jesus. He did so because he looked on his religion as a fulfilment of Christianity and Judaism. He accepted most of the Bible as an earlier revelation of Allah. He called Abraham the first Moslem and Moses, David, and Jesus great prophets. At first his followers faced Jerusalem, not Mecca, and kept the Jewish Day of Atonement, not Ramadan. But neither Jews or Christians could accept much of his teaching and refused to acknowledge him. Muhammad was very disappointed and persecuted the Jews in Arabia, but he still referred to Jews and Christians as *The People of the Book* (the Bible). Later, as the Moslem empire spread, they were treated with special tolerance.

In 1,300 years many sects and movements have arisen but none has destroyed the unity of the Moslem world. One sect of particular interest today is the Ismailis. One branch of the Ismailis accepts as spiritual leader the Aga Khan, who traces his descent back to Muhammad. There are millions of Ismaili Moslems throughout the world, mainly in India, Pakistan, and East Africa. The Aga Khan travels in these countries visiting his followers.

Five times a day the same prayers are said in Islam in exactly the same way. We can understand that some Moslems began to feel that this formal method of praying did not fully express their own experience of God. So certain of them traveled about telling people about the experience they had of God's love and companionship. At the same time they condemned the rich and powerful in society who neglected religion altogether. These teachers were called Sufi because they wore coarse garments of wool (*suf*).

At first they were bitterly persecuted, but later, through the influence of a brilliant scholar, al-Ghazali, their teaching was generally accepted. As a result, brotherhoods of Moslems were formed to seek God through meditation together. Personal devotion was encouraged through the use of prayer beads and the recitation of various beautiful names for God.

Today, pilgrimages are made to the tombs of the Sufis, who are regarded as saints, and their lives and teachings are

studied. One of the most distinguished of them was the Persian poet, Rumi, whose poetry declaring a love of God and concern for all living creatures is still widely read and recited.

Sufism gave rise eventually to a number of strange practices. You might like to look up the history of "The Whirling Dervishes," a sect that developed from this movement in Islam.

But twentieth-century progress poses many new problems for Islam. For a man to have four wives, women to wear veils, prayers to be made five times a day, fasts to be endured for weeks on end—these customs may have suited the leisurely life of long ago, but how can they fit into modern city life? More serious still, Islamic customs caused great areas of arable land to run to waste. With growing populations, this situation became intolerable.

Turkey, a very orthodox Moslem country, gave the lead. Suddenly in 1928 it startled the world by becoming a *secular* state. Sweeping changes took place. Religion no longer decided political and economic policy. The teaching of religion and the Arabic language was prohibited in schools. Religious orders were abolished and public prayer limited. Women were freed from the veil and given equal status with men, and Moslems and non-Moslems were treated alike. Great land reforms were undertaken.

Other Moslem countries followed suit, though it was felt that Turkey had gone too far. Egypt is gradually adopting a modern way of life but does not intend to become a secular state. *"Islam shall be the official religion of The United Arab Republic,"* declares the recent constitution.

But changes are coming, if only in a small way. Where women are not free, a lighter veil is replacing the old heavy one; minarets are wired for loudspeakers. In Tunisia it is decreed that soldiers and children may eat during the Fast of Ramadan.

Students of the Koran say that Muhammad would not have allowed a man more than one wife today and that it is permissible to devise other means of daily prayer.

Though Islam will change, it is unlikely to decline. Moslem nations growing independent and self-conscious do not turn to foreign religions, and they dislike atheism. Muhammad is their prophet, the Koran their Scriptures. Missionary work makes converts for Islam in Africa.

Muhammad in his last sermon declared, *"Know ye that every Moslem is a brother to every other Moslem and that ye are now one great brotherhood."* Though ancient customs disappear, this sense of unity remains and grows.

SIKHS 9

Ban on turbans and beards!

This news item some time ago brought Sikh leaders hurrying from all over Britain to a meeting of protest against religious persecution. A Transport Committee had insisted that Sikh bus crews remove their turbans and beards if they were to work for the city. But no true Sikh could accept these demands.

There are five ancient regulations every Sikh must observe. He must grow his hair long—for which a turban is necessary— he must wear a wooden comb, a steel bangle, shorts (usually covered by trousers) and a small steel knife.

Most of the eight million Sikhs in the world can follow these regulations for they live together in the Punjab in northwestern India. It is a dry country but, owing to irrigation, very fertile. There are so many Sikhs in this part of India that they have been pleading with the Indian government for a state of their own, but so far unsuccessfully.

The word Sikh means "disciple," and Sikhs are disciples of their founder, Nanak, who lived in India from 1469 to 1538. He was a man of remarkable vision.

He dreamed that he could unite two religions that for centuries had been opposed to each other, Hinduism and Islam. As a Hindu, he hated the caste system and the way in which women were treated as inferior to men. Like the Moslems, he believed that there was only one god. He aimed to combine the best in each religion and persuaded his fellow countrymen to accept it. To give practical effect to his teaching, he wore the

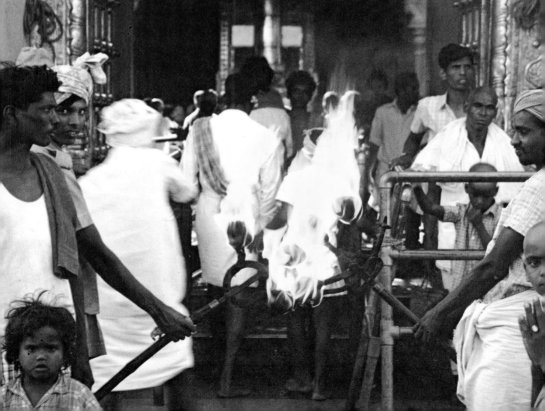

yellow robe of a Hindu holy man and the turban and prayer beads of a Moslem.

He taught that life should be devoted to the love and service of the one supreme god. His followers were to be serious and self-disciplined: no alcohol, no tobacco, and a cold bath each day before early morning prayer.

Why then did a peace-loving people later rank among the best fighters in the world? The Sikhs were driven to take up arms in self-defense. In the seventeenth century they were so bitterly persecuted and humiliated by the Moslems that they vowed it should never happen again. Each man took Singh, meaning "lion," as an additional name, and they called in French officers to teach them to fight.

By the next century they had produced a splendid fighting force of 120,000 men. With it they stopped effectively the Moslem persecutions and later nearly defeated the British. After that they became firm friends of Britain and produced first-class men and officers who fought in both world wars.

The Sikhs have many fine temples. The most beautiful of all is the one built in Amritsar. Its golden domes reflect in the shimmering waters of the lake on which it is built. Every morning the Sikh Scriptures, the Adi Granth, are carried into the temple and chanted by a succession of readers throughout the day.

Sikhs believe that Nanak and all their later teachers were perfect and that, if they aim at perfection themselves, they will be united with them in the next life.

CONCLUSION 10

Gautama, the founder of Buddhism, was one day very much troubled by some of his followers who persistently argued about religion until they almost came to blows. Thereupon he told them this story.

A certain rajah, who was also troubled by quarrelsome teachers and wished to teach them a lesson, invited all the blind men in the neighborhood to visit him. When they were assembled, he had an elephant brought to them. Each of them was invited to describe it. After they had examind it for a few minutes he called them to him. "Now," he said, "what is this thing we call an elephant?"

Those who had examined the top of his head said it was like a great pot; those who had grasped its trunk said it was a plow; those who had felt a leg said it was a kind of pillar; and those who had inspected the end of its tail said it was a broom. Eventually they began to quarrel and aim blows at one another because each refused to accept the others' opinions.

Had they only listened to one another and pooled their knowledge they might have come much nearer to the truth.

This is, in fact, what we are trying to do with the vast subject of religion. In past centuries people of different religions quarreled and fought one another; today we seldom fight, and the wisest, at least, listen to one another and thereby come nearer to the truth. *"Different creeds,"* said the Indian teacher, Sri Ramakrishna, *"are but different paths to reach the Almighty. Every religion is but one of such paths that lead to God."*

We may believe that our own religion has more of the truth than any other—and we may be right—but that should not prevent us from learning something from other faiths.

Most religions, we discover, are concerned about the same things. It is surprising, for instance, how much agreement there is on moral teaching. Read again the Ten Commandments of the Jewish and Christian religions (Exodus 20) and discover how many of them are taught by other religions.

Yet what other religions add to them is also important. Think, for example, of the concern for all living creatures taught by Hinduism and Buddhism or the prohibition of intoxicants and drugs by Buddhism and Islam. Can you improve in matters of honesty on the simple direction, "Do not take that which is not given?" So, by comparison we can discover what standards of conduct are generally acceptable, and by discussion hammer out the principles of a right way of life for ourselves and society.

In still more important matters world religions show remarkable agreement. Allah, God, Brahman are all different names men give to the unchanging reality behind our ever-changing universe. Heaven, paradise, nirvana again are different names given to our experience of union with that reality.

Even the various ways by which men achieve that union have much in common. They all demand self-discipline (to the point of selflessness) and determined effort. No religion says, "Sit back and God will do it for you."

When some Chinese sent to Buddha for copies of the Scriptures he sent them a parcel of blank scrolls. When they became indignant, he smiled. *"These blank scrolls are the true Scriptures,"* he said, *"but if you are so ignorant that you cannot understand, I will put some words on them for you."* He meant, of course, that at best, words can only serve as a map or plan. The task of breaking through to enlightenment can only be done by ourselves.

There are people who say that all this talk about religion and spiritual enlightenment should be a thing of the past. We are now living in a scientific world, and science will answer all our questions and meet all our needs.

This is a bold claim and perhaps those who make it should listen to the story of the blind men and the elephant. The truth about man is so complex that there are many different ways of approaching it. The founder of Christianity once said, *"Man shall not live by bread alone,"* and man's perpetual discontent with himself seems to prove it.

He really lives in two worlds: an outer world of material things and an inner world of thought and feeling. He cannot afford to neglect either. Contentment of mind is worth far more than many journeys to the moon.

Our modern scientific training is helping us to remove much of the dead wood of religion: the superstitions and myths that have grown up over the centuries and obscured the truth. For this we should be thankful, for now we see more clearly what each religion has to teach.

Basically it is this: man's greatest problem is himself, and only within himself can he find the solution he is looking for and needs. There, if he persists, he will discover the true light—be it God, Eternal Spirit, or whatever men call it— which will make clear to him the meaning of his life and the path he should take.

The evidence for this enlightenment is abundant. We should examine it and test it for ourselves.